GREAT PICTURES

AND THEIR STORIES

How To Look At Pictures

"You must look at pictures studiously, earnestly, honestly. It will take years before you come to a full appreciation of art; but when at last you have it, you will be possessed of the purest, loftiest and most ennobling pleasures that the civilized world can offer you."

JOHN C. VAN DYKE.

ST.
AA
PRESS

GREAT PICTURES
AND THEIR STORIES

INTERPRETING
MASTERPIECES
TO CHILDREN

BY
KATHERINE MORRIS LESTER

BOOK FIVE

St. Augustine Academy Press

This book was originally published in 1927
by Mentzer, Bush & Company.

This facsimile edition reprinted in 2024
with improved color images
by St. Augustine Academy Press.

ISBN: 978-1-64051-148-4

CONTENTS

INDEX OF ILLUSTRATIONS IN GREAT PICTURES AND THEIR STORIES

FOREWORD

Picture Study is rapidly becoming an important factor in our public school education. "Nearly every progressive city," says the Bureau of Education, Washington, D. C., "is making use of some form of picture study in the public school system."

The twentieth century has ushered in the reproduction of masterpieces in colors! To what heights of delight the children of the public schools may be carried by the famous pictures of the world in color!

It remains only for the elders to choose pictures adapted to the childish interests; pictures which will cultivate a taste for the best in art; pictures which through the impressionable early years will lead to a true understanding and appreciation of the world's masterpieces!

In preparing this series of readers it has been the aim of those selecting the pictures to consider always the child interest. The field of pictures is large. Not only have the "old masters" been drawn upon, but masters in modern art as well, including modern American artists. Thus constantly, through this series of pictures, the principles of beauty which made possible the "old masters" of yesterday are seen again in the art of today.

In the preparation of the text the child's interest and his ability to read are carefully considered. Real picture knowledge is conveyed in the child's own language.

In the primary grades the interest is largely in "what it is all about." Consequently the text aims to satisfy this curiosity, and at the same time lead to unconscious observation of those things which are most alive to the little child,—color, life, action.

The vocabulary for Books I, II, and III is based on "The Reading Vocabulary," * the Horn, Horn, and Packer List.

*See twenty-fourth Year Book, National Society for the Study of Education, Part I, 1925.

In the intermediate grades, a lively interest in the story is always uppermost. Gradually an appreciation of picture-pattern develops. Simple elements in picture making,—i.e. center of interest, repetition of line and color,—may be intelligently comprehended by children of the intermediate grades.

In the grammar grades great interest in the story continues, and with this interest there develops an appreciation of HOW the story is told,—the real ART of the picture. The pupil not only learns that the picture is a masterpiece, but WHY. He thus acquires standards for judging other pictures.

Each picture is followed by a short sketch of the artist, told in a key adapted to the age and interest of the pupil.

The questions which follow the text will assist in developing an intelligent appreciation of the picture.

The author is particularly indebted to Miss Jennie Long, recently Supervisor of Primary

Education, Peoria Public Schools, for valuable criticism of the primary text. Grateful acknowledgment is also made for the opportunity of practical work with a selected number of primary stories in the schools of Peoria.

The manuscripts of the intermediate and grammar grade books have been submitted to teachers of these grades, to whom the author is indebted for helpful practical suggestions.

The MUSICAL SELECTIONS for the pictures have been graciously contributed by Eva G. Kidder, Director of Music, Peoria Public Schools. The author believes this to be a very valuable feature of these books.

KATHERINE MORRIS LESTER.

ILLUSTRATED WITH REPRO-
DUCTIONS IN COLOR FROM
THE ORIGINAL MASTER-
PIECES, BY COURTESY OF
THE ART EXTENSION
SOCIETY OF NEW YORK.

SPRING DANCE
Breslau Gallery

ARTIST: Franz von Stuck
SCHOOL: German
DATES: 1863-1928

SPRING DANCE

"Ring ting! It is the merry springtime!
How full of heart a body feels!
Sing hey, trolly, lolly,
Oh to live is to be jolly!
When springtime cometh with
The summer at her heels!"*

Air and sunlight! Dance and song! This is the spirit of spring! Blue skies! Leafy trees! Laughing buttercups and daffodils! Oh, to live is to be jolly

When springtime cometh with
The summer at her heels!

So sang our maidens, every one, as they skipped far away from the life of the world to the high green hill-tops beyond. Here they sing and dance, and dance and sing, with sunshine in their waving hair, and flowers at their feet!

*James Bennet, "The Master Skylark." The Century Company, 1897.

13

Poets, artists, and musicians alike love to sing of the spirit of spring. It is a story each one tells just as he likes, but no two stories are ever the same.

One modern painter, Frans von Stuck, has told his story of spring as it has never been told before. He knows the happy season is just beginning. He knows it is the youth of the year. He knows all nature is waking to life. Everything is new. Everything is fresh.

All his colors are as light and airy as the gay young figures sporting about. The trees are a light leafy green. The sky is a delicate blue. The clouds are airy and light. Even the distance is o'erspread with a delicate haze.

Early golden buttercups are laughing in the bright green grass. Above dance the gay, lithesome maidens in tints of green, yellow, and violet. The whole scene is enveloped in the soft, delicate atmosphere of early spring.

While the figures frolic about, notice how the trees, the clouds, and the distant hills swing in the tune of their dance. The tree, at the left, leans with the two figures nearest; that at the right turns its leafy branches echoing the figure in violet. Even the clouds take on the curves of the dancers. The artist has left a rift of blue above which repeats, with outstretched arm, the maiden below. Thus the artist makes all the parts of his picture swing together. It is this that makes rhythm, and gives music to the whole scene.

The painter added a touch of brilliant red to the picture. This gives a beautiful strong note to the spring song. It helps to keep the dancers down to earth; otherwise they might go flitting off to the clouds, so light and airy are they. This brilliant note serves as a happy contrast to the bright pretty green of the hilltop. Notice that it is repeated ever so little, at the left and right, in the subtle suggestion of flowers.

"Oh to live is to be jolly!
When springtime cometh with
The summer at her heels!"

THE ARTIST

Frans von Stuck is known as the "Painter of Fancies." His imagination creates the most fascinating pictures.

In many of his paintings jolly little satyrs and frisky fauns caper and dance about; centaurs play all sorts of pranks on each other; maidens and satyrs alike are joyous and gay, as they swing to the breeze.

Today Frans von Stuck is one of

16

the master-painters of Germany. His pictures are constantly seen in the great exhibitions of Europe.

The story of this little German boy, who grew to be one of the great artists of today, reads like an old-time fairy-tale.

As a little boy he played and worked about his father's mill in a small village in Germany. His father was a miller by trade, and like many other fathers, wanted his son to grow up and become an excellent miller like himself.

"My father would not hear of art," said the painter one day, "He wished me to be a miller."

The father, however, had no idea of the many strange fancies growing in the mind of the little lad. When the boy was very young he began to draw. "I began," he said, "by making child-drawings on the floor with chalk. Then I would amuse myself by making sketches on the family doors." From the very first, you see, Frans von Stuck wanted to be an artist!

Although the father saw nothing but the miller's trade for the boy, the mother had a different idea. She knew her son had talent. She liked his little sketches and constantly encouraged him in his drawing. She wanted him to develop his natural ability. In short, she wanted him to become an artist.

Consequently, when he was twelve years old he left his home in the country and went to a near-by city for the purpose of study. Soon he was attending a school for Industrial Art.

This was a school that prepared young people for work in the great industries of Germany. Here they were taught drawing and design. They were given practice in designing wallpaper, carpets, textiles, and other products manufactured in Germany.

When these same young people started to work in the industries they found that the instruction they had received in the art school gave them a fine preparation for business.

Young von Stuck was delighted with his work in the school. The training was just the kind of instruction he wanted. He would sit for hours making careful outline drawings of various objects.

Here he received a training that stayed with him always. Here he laid the foundation that later made him a master in line-drawing.

In that day many of the boys in the school supported themselves as best they could. Young von Stuck, like the rest, instead of waiting for money from home, set about to earn his living.

"I turned my hand to anything," said he. "I painted plates, made posters, and menu cards and sent sketches to the German comic papers. Sometimes I got only a mark for a drawing but I kept right on."

These drawings were illustrations. So, you see, Frans von Stuck really began his career as an illustrator.

After drawing as an illustrator for some time, the artist introduced color into his pictures. Then it was that he began to make a name for himself!

People began to talk about the color schemes of the artist. Some praised his fine line-drawings, and others the way he combined form and color in composition, or design.

Before this time, German art had been dry, drab, and uninteresting. The work of the artist was so new that a few, who still liked the older style, shook their heads. They did not quite understand these new ideas in color and design.

One day, however, the artist sent his first picture to an exhibition. He was awarded the medal!

From that time on, people began to realize that a great artist had come to modern Germany.

Although Frans von Stuck studied in the best schools of Germany, he says that his style in painting is distinctly his own, that it came to him from no schools and no masters.

When asked how he happens to paint certain pictures, he says he really does not know. Sometimes when looking upon a flower, a picture is suggested to his mind, sometimes a sunset will have the same effect.

Never does this artist paint a scene exactly as it appears. Always, it is his imagination that changes the picture into a design or pattern. The imagination of the artist seems to play over his picture, arranging this part and that, as pleases his fancy, until the whole swings together in pattern.

Like many artists von Stuck is also gifted as a sculptor. One day when asked who taught him sculpture, he replied, "No one. I taught myself. Or if you will, like painting, it came to me."

All through the art of this gifted painter is the note of beauty. Sometimes it is a deep mysterious beauty. Sometimes it is a joyous, rollicking, care-free beauty, as in our picture,— "Spring Dance." Always this beauty is the expression of his artistic imagination.

DIRECTED STUDY

1. Who painted the "Spring Dance"?
   Where does he live?
   What kind of pictures does he paint?

2. What season is represented?
   How do you know?
   What is nature's color at this time?
   Do you think the artist has chosen his colors well? Why?

3. Name the color of sky. Ground. Distance. Trees.
   Are these colors in tune with the time of year?

4. How many dancing figures do you see?
   Name the colors they wear.
   Which do you like best. Why?

5. Why does the tree to the left bend?
   How do the tree and rock to the right curve? Why?

6. Why has the note of red been added? Where is it repeated?
   Does it add beauty to the painting?

7. Is there music in the picture? Where?
   Is there joy in the picture? Where?

8. Do you like this picture? Why?

Related Music: RUSTLE OF SPRING....
................*Sinding*

TO SPRING ....*Grieg*

SPRING SONG *Mendelssohn*

AFTER A SUMMER SHOWER
Art Institute, Chicago

ARTIST: George Inness
SCHOOL: American
DATES: 1825-1894

AFTER A SUMMER SHOWER

A summer shower and then the rainbow! The clouds break and roll away, letting in the bright golden sunlight! The fields turn yellow. The sky turns blue. The tree tops, laden with heavy drops of summer rain, sparkle yellow-green.

What a pretty picture is within the curved arch of the rainbow! See how the clouds fill out the curve of the arching bow! See how the round tree tops echo the curve! Even the rugged old tree and its foliage fall in with the arch of the glowing bow. Within the bow the air is fresh and clear.

The wide stretch of green field is still wet with the summer rain. Here and there a few sheep are grazing in the rich grass. Bits of tree wood lie about. It is very still. Nothing stirs. Here nature waits patiently for the bright warm rays of the summer sun. Soon the dark gray cloud, edging the rainbow, will vanish! Then the whole field will smile a welcome to the glow of yellow sunlight.

The artist framed his picture within the rainbow. The broken edge of the path leads to the trees in the middle distance. Here is the "center of interest."

See how the artist fills this part of the picture with light. Here are the trees! They are not alike, to be sure. A number are grouped into a rounded mass of green. See their trunks! Can you tell how many trees there are?

The trunk of the old rugged tree makes a clear-cut outline against the sky. Its leafy foliage is like fine lace against the yellow-tinted cloud.

Notice how the trees grow smaller and smaller as they lead toward the horizon. This gives distance to the picture. The light roof of the little house with the sky behind it, helps to make the distance seem far away. O yes; it is a long, long way over the field to the little house!

Under the arch is where the sun is shining! Here is where the soft edges of the trees and clouds are tinted with yellow light. Here is where the atmosphere is clear and bright. Here is where the sun is shining after the summer shower!

THE ARTIST

George Inness is America's greatest landscape painter. He is called the "Father of American Landscape." Not only is he the greatest landscape painter of America, but he is one of the great landscape painters of the world. He painted "After a Summer Shower" during the last year of his life, in 1894. It now hangs in the Chicago Art Institute. Here one large gallery has been dedicated to George Inness. It is called the "Inness Gallery." It contains twenty-one of his beautiful landscapes, painted at different periods of his life.

George Inness was born and reared on a farm in New York state. As a child he was sent to the town school. Here he was the despair of his teachers. He showed no interest whatever in arithmetic and grammar! Instead he covered his books with drawings!

Later, thinking to interest the lad in business, his father bought him a grocery store. But Inness remained in the shop only a month. He wanted to paint! He wanted to draw! His world lay not in a grocery store!

Finally the father consented to give the boy lessons in drawing. Accordingly, the best teacher in the town was engaged. It was not long, however, until the teacher found that George knew as much about drawing as did he. In fact, he confessed that he could teach him nothing more.

By and by George made up his

mind to leave business forever, and become a painter.

His father was not pleased over his son's choice of a profession. Nevertheless he permitted George to "follow his bent," and patiently awaited the result.

Inness began immediately to study painting with a French landscape painter. He was now twenty years old. This was the first real instruction he had had in the use of color. It served, however, only as an introduction to painting, for he soon left the studio and started out for himself. During all the rest of his life, nearly half a century, he studied all alone. Once upon being asked whether he ever took any pupils, he replied: "I have had one for a long time, and he is more than enough for me. The more I teach him, the less he knows; and the older he grows the farther he is from what he ought to be."

Inness devoted himself to the study and observation of nature in all her moods. He studied the storm, the calm, the sunshine, and the rain. He studied the effects of all these moods upon the earth, the sky, the clouds, the trees. He put his feeling about it into every landscape. It is his way of painting these moods of nature that makes his landscapes masterpieces of art.

DIRECTED STUDY

1. What is the season of the year?
   What has happened?

2. How is the picture framed in?
   How does the artist give distance to his picture?
   How does he lead into his picture?

3. Where is the "center of interest"?
   How is it accented?
   Do you find any echoing curves?
   Where?
   How does this add to the picture?

4. Name the warm colors.
   Name the cool colors.

5. What "feeling" of atmosphere and
   nature is the artist expressing?

6. Who is the artist?
   When did he live?
   What did he aim to express in his
   landscape painting?
   How does he rank as a painter?

Related Music: THE CALM
   ......*Wm. Tell Overture*

   WITH VERDURE CLAD
   ....*Haydn*

   THE RAINBOW DRESS

THE SEWING SCHOOL
Rijksmuseum, Amsterdam

ARTIST: Constant Artz
SCHOOL: Dutch
DATES: 1837-1890

THE SEWING SCHOOL

*Orphanage at Katwyk**

See the pretty room! It is a typical Dutch interior. Such rooms are found only in Holland.

See the blue china on the cupboard! See the blue tile chimneypiece! This same blue tile is continued around the base of the room. Only in Holland is blue tile used so freely!

This is a home for the orphan children of Holland. It is called an "orphanage." Here the children learn many interesting things.

This is a sewing class. One little girl is showing her work to the teacher. The others are busy with their needles.

They wear little white caps, light aprons, and dark dresses.

---

*Katwyk, a watering-place in south Holland, 23 miles southwest of Amsterdam.

See the odd furniture! Against the back wall is a tall Dutch cupboard. Beside it is a little stand. Only a corner of the fireplace is seen. A clock, with a swinging pendulum, hangs on the side wall. It is 4 o'clock. Late afternoon, you see, is when the shadows are growing long.

See the shining table! It is a square table. The little stool has square corners, too. The room, also, has its square corner. The corner of the table echoes the corner of the room. The corner of the stool echoes the corner of the table. Oh, yes, the artist thought much about his echoing lines!

The little straight-backed chair, the straight edges of the cupboard, fireplace, and curtains, echo the vertical corner of the room.

Notice the long lines of the ceiling beams, floor matting, and window ledge. These give depth to the room.

The little group sits in the bright-

est light about the table. The glowing table reflects its light upon the
white kerchief and cap of the teacher,
making her the most important in
the group.

See the pretty curve made by the
line of white caps! Beginning at the
left, it swings from head to head; one,
two, three, four; then round the
shoulder, and down the arm of the
little girl at the right; across the stool,
and back again to the first little girl.
Round and round goes the line, form-
ing an ellipse, with the white caps
framing the upper edge.

The painter places the group in the
highest light, and gives it the darkest color. Indeed, an artist finds many
ways to emphasize his "center of
interest!"

Do you notice that the dark color
of the dresses is repeated, in a lighter
tone, in the ceiling, the shadows, and
the furniture? Do you notice that the
cool blue-gray shadows, on the aprons,

are repeated in a lighter tone on the wall? The artist thought much about placing his "lights" and "darks" in the picture.

The dark stand with the little picture above, and the dark corner of the fireplace serve as a note of balance to the "center of interest."

Do you see the soft, dark shadows cast on the wall and floor?

The artist has painted so well the effect of the afternoon sun coming through the window, and the soft lights and shadows, that this painting has come to be one of the famous pictures of Holland.

Surely the artist who painted this beautiful Dutch interior lived in Holland! Yes, indeed, he was born in Holland. His name is Constant Artz. He is one of the great modern painters of Holland. Today this picture hangs in the gallery at Amsterdam. In this same city, years before, the artist had won his first great success.

THE STORY OF THE ARTIST

"Every day people in their every day ways is all that can appeal to my heart and eye," so wrote Constant Artz, the Dutch painter, to a friend in England. It is for his beautiful pictures of the Dutch people, — "every day people in their every day ways," —that this artist has won fame.

David Adolphe Constant Artz was born at the Hague, December, 1837. Here he lived until he was about eight years old, then he moved to the large city of Amsterdam.

When he was a mere child he showed great talent for drawing. His family, however, were poor and could not afford to give the little boy drawing lessons.

Later he went to night school where he had a little instruction in drawing. This helped him so much that by the time he was eighteen he drew very well. Indeed, so unusual was his talent that before long he was admitted to the great art school of Amsterdam.

This made him very happy. This was the beginning of his great success.

Every year his paintings became more and more popular, not only in Holland, but in England and France as well.

In Holland he spent his winters at the Hague, and his summers on the dunes at Katwyk, overlooking the sea.

In 1880 he sent this picture,—"The Sewing School," or "The Orphanage at Katwyk," as it is sometimes called, to the Paris exhibition, where it received *Honorable Mention*. This is his most famous picture.

Artz loved the picturesque Dutch people. All his paintings picture the "every day people in their every day ways," for they alone spoke to the "heart and eye" of this happy painter of Holland.

DIRECTED STUDY

1. Where is this pretty room?
   What makes it cheery?
   Whence comes the light?
   Why are the shadows long?

2. Where is the brightest light?
   Where is the darkest color?
   What effect does this have on the picture pattern?

3. How is the "center of interest" arranged?
   How is it emphasized?

4. What lines repeat the vertical lines of the room?
   What lines give depth?

5. How has the artist repeated his color?
   What effect does this give?

6. Who is the artist?
   What kind of pictures appeal to his "heart and eye"?

Related Music: ANDANTE CANTABILE
. . . . *Tschaikowsky*

RUSSIAN WINTER
Private Collection

ARTIST: Igor Grabar
SCHOOL: Russian
DATES: 1871-1960

RUSSIAN WINTER

The "white winters" of Russia are long and cold. In the country districts about Moscow and Leningrad, the scattered homes of the peasants tell of their hardy living. Little and low, with their roofs occasionally red, they give a warm and cheery aspect to an otherwise dreary landscape.

The painter of "Russian Winter" lived in a little village outside Moscow. He knew the country well. He knew the Russian peasant and his labors. He had seen many winters when the blanket of snow lay over the ground for months. His sensitive eye had discovered that snow is not always white. Instead he found it taking on all the tints of surrounding light and color. Sometimes it was warm with a rosy glow; sometimes delicate yellow; sometimes cool blue. To him snow covered Russian country made beautiful pictures!

See the stretch of sunlit Russian snow! The artist carries his distance to the very tip-top of the picture. At the upper left is a group of peasant houses. They are snuggling down in the snow behind the rolling landscape. Their red roofs, among the snow-decked trees, give little notes of warmth and cheer. Opposite, at the end of the path, sits a little house. At the left, tall leafless trees with warm gray-red trunks frame in the picture. And there on a path, directly across the picture, strides a peasant woman!

How soft and downy is the snow in the upper part of the picture! It is warm with sunlight and the reflected tints of red and yellow.

Have you noticed that the houses, pathway, and peasant woman are placed in the upper part of the picture? More than half the painting is foreground,—a wide sweep of snow.

But what a beautiful foreground

it makes! See the delicate tracery of blue shadows! From the lower right of the canvas it grows. Its wandering tendrils spread in a dainty pattern, wider and wider, finer and finer, leading up to the line of the path, and even beyond.

These delicate lines of pattern carry the eye up and on to the picturesque figure of the peasant woman. Surely, there is method in the pattern!

The second road, coming down as it does, keeps our interest here upon the striding figure, in red, and blue, and black. Here is the "center of interest." Here the artist has placed his gayest color and sharpest contrast.

How striking is the gay-colored costume! Her striding step, the swing of the buckets, and the bend of the yoke give vigorous movement and spirit to this happy winter scene.

On she swings, this busy peasant

woman! No doubt she will turn to the right and follow the road. Then over the snow to the little red-roofed house!

THE STORY OF THE ARTIST

Igor Grabar is one of the distinguished modern artists of Russia. Though he has painted many kinds of pictures, it is the snow scenes of his native country that are most admired.

Russian art had been backward for centuries. Just about the time that this artist was born, 1871, the artists of Russia were waking up. They were beginning to see color, light, and atmosphere in the world about them. Our lad grew up under this new order. The life of the present, atmosphere, light, and color were the keynotes of his modern world.

As Igor Grabar grew older, he too was inspired by the new ideals which he saw coming into Russian art.

After graduating from the university and expecting to become a lawyer, he changed his mind.

He wanted to draw! He wanted to paint! So, at the age of twenty-five, he entered an art school in Russia.

He studied here for some time. He progressed, however, much faster than the school. One day he made up his mind to find more interesting study. He packed his satchel and set out to see the world.

He wandered over the length and breadth of Europe, studying as he went. Later, he went to Paris. Here, in the year 1900, he attended a great exhibition of pictures. This was the very thing he had been seeking! This was a new inspiration that set his course for the future!

He returned to Russia. He made his home in a little village outside of Moscow. Here he spent all his time in serious study. He painted figures.

He painted landscapes. He painted continuously in the open air, striving to picture the exact effect of atmosphere.

His long effort was crowned with success. Today he is among the foremost painters of Russia.

Grabar concerned himself chiefly with problems of snow painting. He succeeded admirably. His snow pictures are known not only for their downy whiteness, but for the delicate surfaces which catch so easily the reflections of light and color.

DIRECTED STUDY

1. Of what region is this a picture?
   How has the artist divided his canvas?
   Do you like the proportions? Why?

2. Where is the sun? What time is it?
   How do you know?

3. Name the warm colors.
   Name the cool colors.

4. Where are the principal objects
   placed? Why?
   Describe the upper section.
   Describe the foreground.
   Whence come the shadows?
   Do they affect the picture plan?
   How?

5. Where is the "center of interest"?
   How is it emphasized?
   How does the eye travel to the
   distant houses?
   What gives movement to the scene?

6. Who is the artist?
   Where was he born? When?
   What is his particular field?
   In what does he excel?

Related Music: TROIKA (Three Horse
                Sleigh) ......*Tschaikowsky*

RETURN OF THE FISHERMEN
Private Collection

ARTIST: Joaquin Sorolla y Bastida
SCHOOL: Spanish
DATES: 1862-1923

RETURN OF THE FISHERMEN

The sea! Dazzling sunlight! Fishing boats with gay colored sails! Such are the pictures that spread the fame of Sorolla, Spain's greatest modern artist.

Here on the sandy beach he set up his easel. He sees only the brilliance of sunlight. He sees only the shapes it makes, and the colors it takes. The shapes and forms of objects are never painted for themselves alone. The artist sees only the way the sunlight glistens upon them and the colors reflected from them.

In our picture three sturdy fishermen are bringing their heavy boat up on the beach. They are wonderfully drawn. It is not the drawing, however, that attracts the eye, but the sunlight upon the figures. There is little distinct but the clear-cut outlines.

How the sunshine lights up the

foremost fisherman! It glistens on his wet flesh. It makes bright patches on his clothes. It turns the old straw hat golden yellow.

See the dark lines of clear-cut shadow cast by his thin legs over the sand! See the reflections in the shallow water! Note how the sunlight plays all over the picture. It is everywhere.

The two sturdy figures in the water push with all their strength, while the foremost fisherman holds the towrope. Soon the boat will be dragged smoothly up over the sand.

The strong, old boat is such as is frequently seen in the coast cities of Spain. Its sails are as gay in color as the sunshine itself.

See the shadow cast by the prow of the boat upon the beach! See the purple-blue shadow on the water! It is the shape and color of these shadows that the watchful eye of the artist seizes. It is these wonderful shadows that make the pattern for his picture.

Although there is only beach, and water, and sky, notice the many shapes and colors made by the sun and the deep shadows.

What a picture it is! First, a bit of sandy beach; next, a sunlit band along the edge; then, the "near" sea, the "far" sea, and the sky!

The sandy beach is a golden brown. The thin wash of the water rolling up on the shore is almost white in the sunlight. The red-gray shadow makes an interesting color contrast on the clear water. Next is the purple-blue shadow cast by the boat. Note its shape. Beyond are the "near" waters, with their foaming crests running off in two lines which meet near the head of the fisherman. Still further beyond is the calm gray sea. Then follows a narrow stretch of silent sky.

Thus the artist carries us over the sea to the distance. But what an interesting sea it is! A sea of sunlight, shadow, and color! A sea made beautiful by its pattern of "dark" and "light!"

Note the colors in the beach, the "near" sea, and the "far" sea. See the color in the fisherman's boat. It seems that all the colors in the picture have been floated together, darkened, and spread upon the old boat! Surely the artist knew how to harmonize his color!

"Sunlight!" is the one word in the art of Sorolla. It produces color. It produces form. It produces the bright, sparkling atmosphere in his pictures of the sea!

THE STORY OF THE ARTIST

Sorolla, the Spanish painter, is one of the greatest of modern artists. He was born in Valencia in 1862. It is this old sea-coast city in Spain that inspired many of his famous pictures.

Although left an orphan when a mere child, he was fortunate in having a very kind uncle. This uncle took the little boy into his own home and looked after him, taking the place of a father.

As soon as the little fellow was old enough to go to school he began to draw. He surprised his teachers by decorating the pages of his book with little drawings. His teachers and uncle alike looked at these little sketches and were much pleased. Yes, the boy had great talent, that was easily seen!

Fortunately the boy's uncle did not discourage him in his drawing. Instead he sent him to a neighboring trade school where he could have the proper instruction.

Here he learned to draw. His teachers were amazed at his skill. They were enthusiastic in their praise of his talent. They advised him to go on with his studies, predicting a great future for him.

After he had learned all he could at

the trade school, he went to the Art Academy in his native town, Valencia. Here, too, his work was considered marvelous.

By this time the little Spanish boy had grown to manhood. Then came the great day when he set up his easel in the wide out-of-doors, and began to paint in a true open-air light.

He saw the shapes or patterns made by the shadows. He saw the many colors made by the sunlight and shadows. He saw the glistening light as it sparkled over the sandy beach and the sea.

As he looked upon the sea, the land, the sky, the sunlight, and the shadows, he painted them just as they appeared.

His first picture painted out-of-doors was a bull fight. He tried to make it as *real* as possible so he grouped his models in a dusty enclosure, and then to give it the appearance of fact, steeped them in smoke. It proved to be a very *real* picture but not a great one. It was however, the beginning of those out-of-door pictures for which he later became the most famous painter in Spain.

Sorolla always kept to his original plan, that is, to make everything as *real* as it appears. Such a painter is called a *realist*.

It was not long before his out-of-door pictures brought him public notice. He won many medals and honors. Then he traveled to Paris and Rome where he spent much time in study. The pictures, painted in these great art centers, brought him fame.

It was Spanish sunlight, however, that brought him the greatest success. The Spanish sunlight playing over the waters about Valencia made him love the sea and the life upon it. All the scenes and incidents connected with the fisher-folk of his own country captivated him. He liked to see them out upon the beach in their old fishing boats of many colors. He liked to see these rugged men of the sea pulling in their well-laden nets, or preparing to set out for the day's work.

Always it was out upon the beach that he set up his easel. There, with the sparkling light upon the scene, he painted with strong vigorous strokes the picture before him just as it appeared.

The artist had no use for an in-door studio. Many times he laughingly said, "A studio is useless in the equipment of a painter, his workshop being out of doors in the full sunlight where the wind blows."

So great has been the fame of Sorolla that in February 1909 an exhibition of his paintings was held in America. Three hundred pictures were sent from Spain to New York City. The artist himself came all the way to America to superintend the hanging of his pictures. Great was the enthusiasm of the public in seeing, not only the pictures of this famous painter, but also the artist himself at the exhibit.

Crowds visited the exhibition. Sorolla became the idol of the art-loving public.

When the pictures were brought to this country, it was understood that they were intended for exhibition purposes only and would be sent back to Spain. Anyone who wanted to buy a Sorolla painting was obliged to file application with the United States custom authorities. Within a short time every painting in the exhibition was on file!

The success of the exhibition was extraordinary. The records showed that 159,831 persons attended. Sorolla himself was delighted with the reception his work received in this country.

We are not surprised to read that this artist while at the height of his success became court painter to the king of Spain and lived part of the time in the Spanish capital, the city of Madrid.

Sunshine is the word that sums up the success of Sorolla. "He was born with sunshine in his heart," exclaimed a friend.

DIRECTED STUDY

1. What is the picture's most interesting feature?
   How much is beach? Sea? Sky?

2. Where is the sun? How do you know?
   Can you tell the time of day?
   How does the sunlight affect the scene?

3. Describe the shapes of shadows on the beach. On the water.
   How do these shapes add to the picture?

4. What is the color of the shadows?
   What is the color of the highest light?

5. Where is the "center of interest"?
What are the fishermen doing?
Why are their outlines clearcut?

6. Describe the play of light on
the wet flesh. On the clothes.
What causes the two dark par-
allel lines on the beach?

7. Name the colors in the boat
and sails.
Where are these colors repeated
in a lighter key?

8. Who is the artist?
Where was he born? When?
Are his pictures real or imag-
inative?
What is the "keynote" of his
art?

Related Music: A SAILOR'S LIFE......
........*Van Tussenbrock*

FISHERMAN'S SONG...
................*Parker*

FISHERMAN'S PRAYER
.... *Myrberg*

THE SONG OF THE LARK
Art Institute, Chicago

ARTIST: Jules Breton
SCHOOL: French
DATES: 1827-1906

THE SONG OF THE LARK

O lark of the summer morning,
  Teach me the song that you sing;
I would learn without lightness or scorning,
  To give praise for every good thing.*

The "Song of the Lark" is one of the most famous paintings in America. It pictures a peasant girl of France going to her work in the fields. With her sickle in hand, she goes to help the reapers. In the distance, far beyond the rough field and the little hamlet, the sun is rising, a flaming disk of molten gold. Slowly it climbs above the distant tree tops. The soft glow of early morning lights up the whole field. It helps to show the roughness of the ground. It helps to show the path along which the peasant girl walks. Soon the whole scene will be flooded with the warm, bright rays

*From the Japanese. The Art Music Readers; Chicago. Mentzer, Bush & Co.

of the sparkling early morning sun.

The dew sparkles on the tender leaves! The birds awake! A lark, trilling its morning song, soars above! The peasant girl catches the notes of the soaring lark. She pauses. A happy smile breaks over her rugged features. The lark's morning message of cheer gives her new happiness. For the moment she is filled with joy.

She stands listening to the morning song. How sturdy and strong she appears! Her life in the great out-of-doors has made her healthy and vigorous. How brown is her face, her hands, her arms! Yes, she has worked in the fields since childhood, and nature has given her a heavy coat of tan.

She wears the coarse clothing of all French peasants. Her dark skirt hangs full. Her blue apron is turned up and fastened at the back. Her simple blouse, with its open neck and rolled sleeves, is comfortable and easy.

Like her peasant sisters she wears her hair bound in a soft cloth.

She walks bare-foot, enjoying the touch of the cool earth. She likes to breathe the early morning air. Many times she has seen the beautiful tinted colors of the morning sky. Now, however, she sees only the lark, and hears only his song. Her heavy peasant face is brightened with joy as she listens.

The artist evidently wanted us to see only the happy peasant girl, for he has kept all else in the picture very, very simple. The field is a mass of brown, the distance a sweep of green. There is little detail. Only a pleasing division of picture space, sky, distance, foreground. Against this background, softly tinted with morning light, the artist placed the sturdy peasant girl, her face alight with happy thoughts.

Notice that the figure of the girl is silhouetted against the brown field and morning sky. See how the atmosphere fills every part of the picture, especially the space back of the girl. The artist made this space appear far distant by making the color softer and softer, and massing the foliage more and more as he painted back into the picture.

Notice the coarse grass and flowers growing in the front of the picture. In the middle distance they become only a mass of color, while in the far distance the outline and softened color merely suggest trees and massed foliage.

Although we see the sky, the field, and roof tops of a distant village, the artist has painted these in quiet masses of color only as a setting for the figure of the peasant maid.

Do you notice that the distance lies in a strong horizontal position? Do you notice that the figure of the peasant girl is a perpendicular line against it?

Horizontal lines always give repose and quiet to a picture. Here, the line of the distance makes one feel the quietness of the early morning. The erect line of the figure gives a feeling of strength to the picture. It helps us to feel the sturdy, vigorous life of the French peasant.

Do you notice that the thought of the girl is centered upon the lark? We, too, follow the gaze of the peasant maid to find, if we can, this bird of the early morning. Although the peasant girl fills the picture, it is the lark that is the "center of interest," for it claims the absorbed attention of the peasant maid, and then our own.

All the pictures painted by this artist are filled with notes of happiness. Although he pictures the hard working peasant, he always tells of the joy he found in his work,—never the labor. So in our picture of this humble peasant girl going through the early morning field to her work, the artist pictured the joy that changed her heavy features to happiness as she listened to the song of the soaring skylark.

THE STORY OF THE ARTIST

Jules Breton is the happy painter of French peasant life. He was not a peasant himself, and knew little of the hard work and dreary life of the French peasant.

He liked, however, to see these fine, strong, figures of men and women in working clothes. He liked to see them working in the fields. He liked to see them returning at evening.

He always selected the happy, the joyous, the healthy, the vigorous, for his pictures. In studying the pictures of Breton's peasants one is led to believe that work is always a joy!

Jules was born in the country of Courrieres, France. His father's house was set in the midst of a beautiful garden, with open fields stretching beyond. Here he and his four brothers roamed about, and played to their hearts' content.

One day when he was a little fellow he watched a painter whitewash some Chinese figures which stood in the garden. He watched him brighten up the decorations in the house. From that day Jules declared he would be a painter.

Not long after a great painter called at their home on business. He came in, and spent some little time with the father. Jules looked on. He wanted, oh so much, to tell him that he, too, wished to be a painter. But he dared not say a word.

Some years later an uncle happened to meet this same painter. He engaged him to paint his portrait. He thought this would bring him to the house where he might become interested in his nephew.

Sure enough he came to the house. He met Jules. He looked at his drawings. He shook his head.

By and by, however, his face brightened when he saw the boy's out-door sketches. He consented to take him on trial for six months.

The young lad was delighted. He ran to his room, threw his school books to the ceiling, and other work into the fire. He was going to have lessons in drawing!

He began studying with this well known painter. This was only the beginning of long years of serious study. Afterward he went to Paris where his training fitted him for the great artist he was to be.

When he returned home, he went out into the country around his boyhood home, the country he loved best. Here were the open fields and the familiar scenes of his childhood.

Breton was a poet as well as a painter. As he strolled through the fields, he sang and whistled as he passed. He saw only the beauties of nature, the blue sky, moving clouds, lights, and shadows. He saw only the beautiful side of French peasant life, —their fine stalwart figures, their strength, and hardiness. To him the harvesters were *always* merry, the gleaners *always* gay, and all the workers contented and happy.

Naturally when he began to paint these workers at their daily toil he pictured only the happiness and joy that he saw.

Immediately his pictures became popular. People liked his paintings because they pictured the bright, happy side of work. He became one of the greatest painters not only in France, but in the whole world.

Many of his celebrated paintings are now in America. His masterpiece, "The Song of the Lark," hangs in the

Art Institute of Chicago. Here, any day one may study the original painting straight from the hand of this great French master. It is much better to see the original than the finest reproduction ever made.

DIRECTED STUDY

1. What time of day is it?
   How do you know?

2. Describe the color of the sky.
   Of the light. Of the ground.

3. Where is the girl going?
   How is she dressed?
   Why does she carry a sickle?

4. What does she hear?
   How does she look?
   How does she feel?

5. Why did the artist place the
   skyline high?
   Would you raise it? Why?
   Would you lower it? Why?

6. Name the principal space-divisions in the picture.

 Do you like the placing of the figure?

 Would you move it?

7. How does the artist give a feeling of space back of the figure?

8. What makes the picture quiet?

 What tells of the strength of the peasant girl?

 Why has the artist kept the background simple?

9. Who is the artist?

 What kind of pictures did he paint?

 Why did people like his pictures?

 Where is the original painting,—"The Song of the Lark"?

Related Music: LO, HERE THE GENTLE LARK .... *Bishop*

HARK, HARK THE LARK .... *Schubert*

MERRY LARK..... *Gounod*

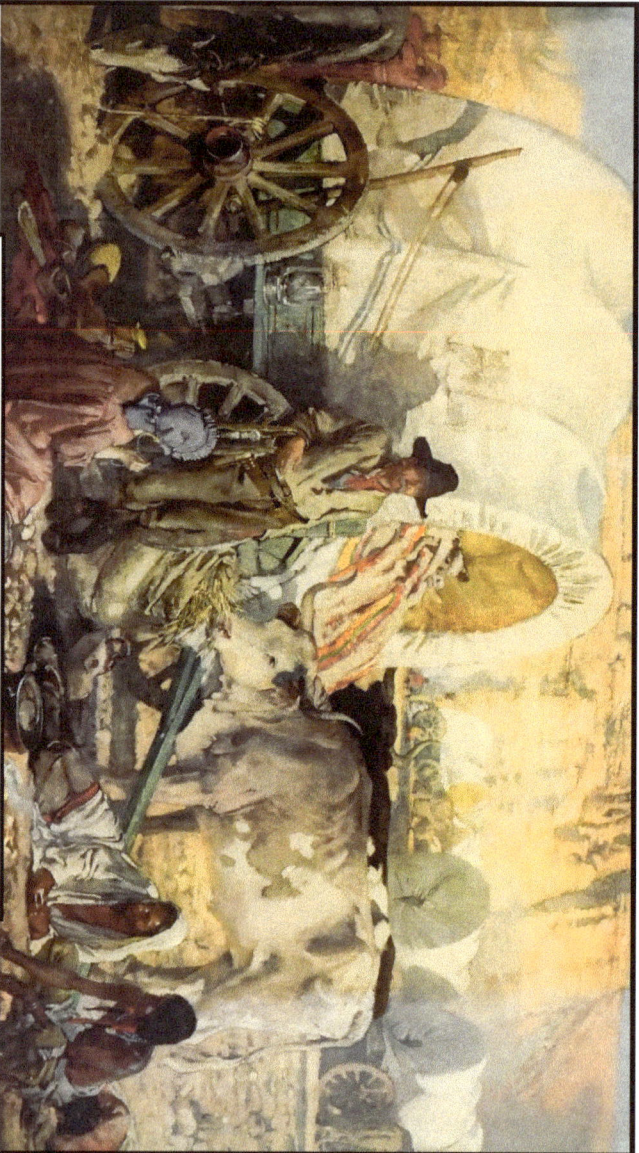

SANTA FE TRAIL
Private Collection

ARTIST: John Young-Hunter
SCHOOL: American
DATES: 1878=1955

THE OLD SANTA FE TRAIL

The story of the great West begins with the "covered wagon." To-day the covered wagon has become the symbol of the early pioneer days.

Then it was that whole families and neighborhoods gathered their possessions together and started for the unknown west. Their covered wagons made a long picturesque line as they trailed their winding way over the great stretch of western plain.

Many were the hardships endured. Many were the fierce attacks of the red man. Sometimes, however, the Indians were friendly, and they and the white man smoked the peacepipe together.

The old Santa Fe trail runs toward the southwest, through New Mexico and the adjoining states. Now the Santa Fe Railroad follows this route.

It is a hot, dry country, full of clear

brilliant, and never-ending sunshine.

See the color of the landscape! The rocks and sand are burned to a brilliant red-orange. There in the distance are the sandstone cliffs. The little openings remind us of the people, who, long ago, lived up there in the shelving rock.

Below, the dry earth takes on the same color. Not a sprig of green! The hot desert is everywhere!

In the midst of all this brilliant sunshine, a rugged pioneer stands leaning against the wheel of his covered wagon. Near him, on the grass, sits his companion. She too has come on this long, long journey. A little further to the right are two friendly Indians. They, perhaps, have come to trade. The heavy ox, with the wide-curving horns, has walked all the way. By this time he feels a part of the family. At the left a horse is quietly nibbling the brush. Lucky is he if he finds a sprig of green in this dry, sunburned country!

Off in the distance are other covered wagons, belonging to the same wagon-train. They have unhitched their horses and camped here for a brief rest.

How very real is the big wagon! It is just like hundreds of others that crossed the western plains. The sun, shining on the white canvas, turns it to yellow. The other wagons, too, have taken on delicate yellow tints.

See the sharp contrast made by the blue and purple shadows against the white canvas!

See how the sun shines on the little group! It throws pretty lace-like shadows on the white shawl of the Indian. It turns the dress and bonnet of the seated woman to reds and browns. Even the ox takes on the warm glow of the sun!

The sturdy pioneer stands in the full sunlight. He wears a rough shirt and broad-rimmed hat. His strong high boots protect his feet and legs. He is, indeed, the typical pioneer of the West. He seems to be the center of the little group, for all are looking toward him. Even the ox stands facing him! Although we look to the right, although we look to the left, although we look to the far distance, we always come back to our rugged pioneer, standing in the full sunlight beside his big covered wagon. So much has been written about the pioneers of the West! So much has been said about the long wagon trains, the desert camps, and the hardships of pioneer life.

Instead of telling it again in words, the artist has told it in picture. He *pictures* the brilliant sunlight. He *pictures* the heat reflected from the sunburned earth. He *pictures* the covered wagon and this sturdy pioneer group. Through picture we learn of the sunlight and life on the old Santa Fe Trail.

THE ARTIST

John Young-Hunter was born in Scotland in 1878. When he was only nineteen years old he won his first recognition as a painter at the Royal Academy, London.

After living in England, he one day came to America. Here he discovered the picturesque country west of the Mississippi. Like many other artists he decided to join the colony of painters at Taos, New Mexico, on the old Santa Fe Trail. Here in the land of the Pueblo Indian he spent many summers.

Taos is a sage-brush desert 7000 feet above sea-level. Beyond the village tower the giant mountains to a height of 13,000 feet. Here the sky is a beautiful turquoise blue. The color is brilliant and vibrating. No wonder that Taos has claimed a whole colony of modern painters!

Over a hundred years ago, in 1826,

the first covered wagon trailed along the old Santa Fe road to Taos. This event was celebrated in 1926 by the pioneers of the village, who dressed themselves in the style of their hardy frontier ancestors and paraded the streets. The Indians, too, in their gay-colored blankets marched along with them. What a parade it was!

Here, too, lived the famous frontiersman, Kit Carson, whose house still stands,—one of the sights of the village. It is said that the artist knew the widow of this noted pioneer, and that she made many suggestions about the arrangement and details of his painting,—"The Old Santa Fe Trail."

This picture was exhibited at the Royal Academy, London.

Today John Young-Hunter is known also as a portrait painter. His pictures hang in the great galleries of the Luxemburg, Paris, and the Tate Gallery, London.

DIRECTED STUDY

1. Where is this sunny land?
   Of what period in American history does it tell?
   When did the first covered wagon pass over this trail?
   What passes over it now?

2. Where is the sunlight in the picture?
   How does it affect the scene?
   Sand? Cliffs? Wagon?

3. Where are the shadows?
   What is their color?

4. What is the "center of interest"? How do you know?
   What group is of secondary interest?

5. Describe the wagon.
   Does the pioneer seem hardy?
   Describe his dress.

6. Who is the artist?
   Where did he paint the picture?

Related Music: Santa Fe Trail.........
........*OH SUSANNAH*

APPEAL TO THE GREAT SPIRIT
Museum of Fine Arts, Boston

ARTIST: Cyrus E. Dallin
SCHOOL: American
DATES: 1861-1944

APPEAL TO THE GREAT SPIRIT

Years ago this great country of North America belonged to the red man. He roamed its broad plains at will. He climbed its rugged mountains. He paddled his canoe over its shining waters. There was nothing to disturb him. But one day the white man came. The white man destined to rule! Gradually, the red man gave up his land, gave up his possessions.

By and by, he looked about him. Behold! This great country with its broad prairies, and shining streams was rapidly becoming the home of another race. This land, once belonging to his people, was passing to the white man.

The white man was strong. They were many in number. The red man looked upon the power and strength of the white man. He saw the end of his own possessions, the end of his race. He knew not where to turn. He was helpless and in utter despair.

The artist who modeled this statue lived among the Indians. He knew the red man well. He knew their feelings. He knew their love of the mountains, prairies, and rivers. He knew, too, that the red man looked to the Great Spirit as the Giver of all this good.

The sad plight of the Indian, bereft of his land, his possessions, and his freedom, touched the mind and heart of the artist. He wanted to picture the Indian's feelings when he looked about him, and saw his vast country in the possession of strangers and his race about to disappear.

His imagination pictured the stalwart figure of the Indian seated upon his friendly steed. He saw him lonely, sad, dejected, thinking upon the passing of his great race. He saw the Indian's horse looking as dejected as the red man himself.

Suddenly the red man sees a ray of hope,—the Great Spirit! He raises his head. He looks up. His lifeless arms begin to rise, and his hands slowly lift themselves beseeching the Great Spirit for help.

How still are the rider and horse! Not a muscle moves. The Indian sits, relaxed, without saddle or stirrup. Notice how the legs hang down over the back of the horse. The toes point down. The arms are extended down and out. The long braids hang down. All is down, down, down. The upturned face and outstretched palms, alone, look up.

Even the horse has caught the spirit of the rider. He, too, stands relaxed. His ears droop. The long tail hangs motionless. The four straight legs and the feet, side by side, show no action or spirit. The reins hang loose. He too, in his mute way, joins with his master in the appeal to the Great Spirit. In this way the artist makes not only *one* figure of horse and rider, but he makes them *one* in their feeling

as well. In this way he gives unity to
his statue.

But after all, the Indian is not
without a ray of hope, for he looks
up, up, and up. The Spirit that has
been his help in the past surely will
not desert him now! The upward
look, the upturned palms, call upon
the Great Spirit as the last hope of
the red man!

It is the upward look, and the upturned palms, alone, that carry the
message of hope. Suppose the head
were bowed, and the arms hanging at
the side. Would this change the picture? Yes, indeed! In such a picture
there could be no hope. This, however, is not the message of the artist.
He wished to tell of the faith and
hope of the Indian, face to face with
defeat.

No other statue in the world ex-
presses the deep feeling of the Indian
as does this. To put feeling like this
into bronze is the work of a master-

artist! Such a one is Cyrus W. Dallin, the American sculptor.

Among his many bronze figures commemorating the life and faith of the red man, none has gained greater fame than this, his recent work, "The Appeal to the Great Spirit."

THE ARTIST

Cyrus W. Dallin was born and reared among the Indians. He knew the red man well. These were the pioneer days, and Dallin's home like those of other pioneers was a log cabin with adobe walls. He says there were two things about his boyhood home that thrilled him. One was the Indians, the other his mother's flower garden.

The Indians were such splendid fellows in their gay trappings, their feathers, and beads, that they won the young sculptor's heart. Many times, no doubt, they stopped at the gay-colored garden of his mother and chatted with her and the boy. Little did they know that this same little boy was destined to make the red man live forever in bronze!

All through this western country great beds of clay abound. Naturally this little western lad easily discovered the great fun of modeling in clay. To model an Indian! To model the Indian's pony! This, was indeed a happy discovery.

It is said that at seven he had modeled the heads of his favorite chiefs. Later, as a lad of eighteen, he was working one day with some miners in a mining camp when they struck a bed of fine white clay. Young Dallin quickly made some tools and immediately set to work on two life-sized figures.

The miners of the camp were so delighted with the boy's work that they determined to help him.

One day they learned that a great fair was to be held in Salt Lake City.

They decided to send several examples of the young sculptor's work to the fair. This was the beginning of his success.

At once, a number of wealthy miners recognized his great talent and sent him to Boston for study.

After several years study in Boston, he had the good fortune to go to Paris. Here he became the friend of the celebrated animal painter, Rosa Bonheur.

While in Paris, Buffalo Bill's show came to the city. This was a great day!

Here were the red men from America! Dressed in their native costumes they paraded the streets of the French capital. Many Parisians had never seen Indians before. They thronged the streets to catch a glimpse of the strange visitors.

Dallin and his friend, Rosa Bonheur, spent many days in study at the Indian camp. The Indians showed great friendship for both Dallin and the French painter.

Just before the show left Paris the two artists visited the camp. Rosa Bonheur carried a little gift with her. This was a ring which she presented to an aged chief as a token of her friendship for the red man. The old chief took the ring, placed it on his finger, and said through an interpreter, "I place this ring on my finger as a sign of friendship and the finger shall leave the hand sooner than the ring."

The result of the sculptor's study in the Indian camp was a life-sized statue called, "The Signal for Peace." It now stands in Lincoln Park, Chicago. The statue pictures the welcome the red man gave to the white man. It was the first of a series of four statues presenting the story of the red man.

The subject of the second is the seer of the tribe,—"The Medicine Man." He sees the end, and tries to warn his people as to what will soon happen.

"The Protest" shows an Indian on horseback, hurling defiance at the white man.

The fourth,—"The Appeal to the Great Spirit,"—pictures the last hope of the red man. This statue now stands before the Museum of Fine Arts, Boston. Here many people stop and admire it every day.

It is said that the educated Indian of today joins with the white man in praise of the sculptor's work.

One day an Indian was seen standing before one of Dallin's figures. Soon he spoke: "This statue at once brings back to my mind the scenes of my early youth—scenes that I shall never again see in reality." Then he added words of praise for the artist who could rise above the petty likes and dislikes of one race for another, and picture the real man beneath the strange exterior.

The secret of Dallin's art is best

understood by reading his own words: "The Indian is to me first of all a human being, with emotions and affections. No one is stronger in friendship, or quicker in appreciation, once you have established yourself in his confidence.

America is proud to claim Cyrus W. Dallin as one of her distinguished modern sculptors, who has made the American Indian live forever in bronze.

DIRECTED STUDY

1. What story does the artist tell?

2. What is the feeling of the Indian?
   How does the artist show this?
   Name the parts of the statue that
      suggest this feeling.

3. How did the artist express hope?
   What parts of the figure express
      hope?

4. Is there any feeling in common between horse and rider? What?
   How has the artist secured unity of figure and horse?

5. Suppose the Indian bowed his head and lowered his hands; would this change the meaning? How?
   Suppose the horse were stepping forward, head up, tail arched; would this change the meaning? How?

6. Who is the artist?
   Where did he live?
   How did he come to know the red man?
   How did he come to model in clay?

   Name other Indian sculptures which are companion to this.
   Where is this statue?
   Do you like it? Why?

Related Music: INDIAN LAMENT. *Dvorak*
FROM AN INDIAN
LODGE ......*MacDowell*

LADY WITH A LUTE
Metropolitan Museum, New York

ARTIST: Jan Vermeer
SCHOOL: Dutch
DATES: 1632-1675

THE LADY WITH A LUTE

A low sweep of strings! A melody, deep and rich, fills the quiet corner of this lighted room. Again and again the strings repeat the strain. The musician listens intently as she looks toward the lighted window.

How quiet, how peaceful the scene! Only the low hum of the strings is heard. The light coming through the pretty leaded window falls directly upon the lady with the lute. It lights up her expressive face. Her pretty yellow jacket trimmed with white fur is the brightest note in the picture. The books and music on the table nearby catch a bit of the reflected light. The back wall takes on a low mellow glow.

This artist, Jan Vermeer of Delft, is celebrated for his painting of light. It is not always sunlight, but often only the light of day, coming through windows and doors, that has made him one of the world's greatest painters.

Here the window is closed. The light as it shines through the glass spreads all over the room. Some objects are thrown into deep shadow, some into half shadow, while the lady herself catches the full light as it comes through the window.

What an interesting room it is! It is a room in a Holland house,—perhaps a house in Delft where the artist lived.

See the big squares of the tile floor! See the massive Dutch furniture! The map hanging on the wall appears in many of this artist's pictures. Vermeer delighted in maps! With the greatest care he drew and painted them. Sometimes he filled the borders with little views seen in the quaint Dutch towns.

Here he fits the map on the upper right wall. Its colors are dark and rich. It breaks the wall space giving the background greater interest.

Notice the accented line of its vertical and horizontal edges. These, you see, are repeated again and again in the door, window, and the furniture of the room. These long horizontal lines help to make us feel that the Dutch room is both quiet and restful.

A curtain hangs at the pretty window. Its color melts into the shadow beside it. See how the artist has painted the soft hazy edge of the shadow! How it merges into the wall! Contrast the edge of the shadow with the edge of the map. Yes, indeed, Jan Vermeer was a master painter!

The heavy Dutch furniture is in deep shadow. The artist has placed the darkest notes in the very front of the picture. The window is close to the wall farther back. The light falls here rather than in the front of the picture. This is quite the reverse from the way pictures are generally painted. Usually the front is more brilliantly lighted; the color grows grayer and grayer as it goes back into the picture. Our picture, however, is painted in the way that the artist liked best. When we think of the pictures of Vermeer, we always think of light and color far back in a room.

Although the furniture is in deep shadow, notice the low, rich light over the chair. How the gleaming nailheads sparkle! Vermeer has a way of touching up these little points of light with the very tip of his brush.

And what shall we say of the lady herself! See the curve of her pretty head against the wall! Her hair is arranged in the fashionable Holland way. The bandeau encircling the head catches a spot of light from the window.

See the earrings! See the string of pearls! Each is touched with a tip of light! This is all beautiful; all exquisitely painted. It is the face, however, with its lovely outline, and the expressive eyes and brow, that win and hold our greatest admiration.

Do you notice that the artist has made the beautiful head the "center of interest"? Not only does the light shine brightest here, but the long lower roll of the map points directly to this part of the picture. The eye follows along this line until it, too, reaches the lovely head of the lady with the lute. Jan Vermeer knew not only how to paint the mellow glow of light, but he knew, too, how to compose his pictures. He knew how to emphasize by light, color, and line the most important part of his picture!

Our lady with the lute continues her low-toned strain. The light plays a deep rich melody over the room. The atmosphere vibrates with the harmony of tone and color.

This beautiful painting, now in the Metropolitan Museum, New York City, is one of the thirteen Vermeers in America. It is one of the highly prized paintings in this country.

THE STORY OF THE ARTIST

Jan Vermeer of Delft is one of the greatest names in Dutch painting. During his lifetime he was known by all the distinguished people in Holland. Shortly after his death, however, he was well nigh forgotten. He remained unknown for centuries. It was only after his name had been discovered signed to an old painting, that the world of today came to know anything about Jan Vermeer.

Now it has been found that, after his death, false names had been signed to the pictures he had painted during his lifetime. These pictures had paraded for years under these false names.

One day, however, when the grime of centuries was being removed from a painting, the name of the artist was found neatly lettered on the background. Since that time many of the original paintings of the artist have very fortunately been recovered.

Today about thirty or forty pictures by Vermeer are known. About one third of this number are in this country.

Because this famous artist was discovered centuries after he had passed away, little is known of his life. We do know, however, that his parents lived in the quaint little town of Delft, and that there Jan was born in 1632. It is impossible to say where he studied or who his teachers may have been.

At this period there were many painters living in Holland and Jan, no doubt, was interested in the work that each was doing. He probably visited them in their studios, chatted with them about their colors, the painting of light, and other things that had to do with the making of pictures. He must have gained something from each of them for his use of light and color resembles that of other artists of that day.

Who his teachers may have been, or where he studied, however, matters little to us of today. We know him as the painter of daylight. His favorite subject was light passing through open doors or windows of a room. Many times the windows are closed, and the light, passing through the glass, is diffused over the room.

The room, the furniture, the wall and the people seem to be bathed in an atmosphere of light. Generally the walls of his rooms are plaster, upon which the atmosphere seems to move. A map or large picture usually breaks the wall space. His figures are always expressive and intent upon what they are doing.

In our picture, "The Lady with a Lute," we find many ideas that are characteristic of all the pictures that Jan Vermeer painted. Here we see the glowing light coming from the left side of the room as it usually does. We see the hazy light on the walls and the deep shadows lurking about the room. We see the sharp edge of the curtain softened by shadow. We see the space of the back wall broken by the map hanging upon it. Against the wall, in the full light, we see the expressive head of the lady intent upon what she is doing. So it usually is in all of Vermeer's paintings.

Perhaps, some day, you may see other pictures of this great Dutch master. If you do, remember to look for the light coming through a window at the left, the map or picture hanging on the wall, and the expressive face of the figure.

There are certain colors, too, which we see again and again in the paintings of this famous master of The Netherlands. His favorite colors are a cool "moonlight blue" and lemon yellow. The yellow tones are seen in the softly illumined walls, the furniture, curtains, and other surfaces in the rooms. Both blue and yellow are seen in the costumes of his figures.

In our painting of the lady playing on the lute, his favorite yellow is seen in the fur-trimmed jacket. In the mellow light on the back wall and in the soft shadows lurking about the room we see the same favorite yellow, toned off, into a warm golden glow.

This master of Delft was a poet in his use of color and light. His deep rich shadows, half lights, and high lights sing together in a harmony like music.

DIRECTED STUDY

1. What is the artist's chief interest in this picture?

2. Where are the darkest shadows? Where is the brightest light? What effect does this give?

3. Describe the effect of light on the wall. The map. The floor. The furniture.

4. How does the artist make the room quiet and restful?

5. What is the dominant color in the picture?
   Where is it brightest?
   Where is it toned off?

6. What is the "center of interest"?
   How do you know?
   Name two ways in which the artist has emphasized it.

7. What is the lady doing? How does she look?
   Describe her dress. Her jewels.
   Is the music gay, soft, loud or low?
   How do you know?

8. Who is the artist?
   For what is he noted?
   Where does this picture hang?
   Do you like it? Why?

Related Music: HOW LOVELY ARE
                THY MESSENGERS. .
                . . . .*Mendelssohn*

GALAHAD THE DELIVERER
Public Library, Boston

ARTIST: Edwin Austin Abbey
SCHOOL: American
DATES: 1852-1911

GALAHAD THE DELIVERER

Sir Galahad was the blameless knight of King Arthur's Round Table. He was destined to succeed in the greatest adventure in the world, the quest of the Holy Grail.

The Holy Grail was a cup of wonder and mystery. It was said to be the cup from which Jesus drank at the Last Supper. It could be seen only by those who were perfect in thought, word, and deed. Moreover it was believed to have strange magical powers. He who succeeded in possessing it could live without food. It gave him all knowledge. It gave him protection in battle. Only the most perfect knight in all the world was worthy to possess it!

The Grail had been hidden for centuries in an enchanted castle called, "The Castle of the Grail." The king of the castle and all his household were held under a magic spell. They could never hope to be free until some knight, perfect in wisdom, should come and break the spell by speaking words of wisdom. This, indeed, was a great adventure!

Galahad as a boy lived in a convent. The nuns had taught him many things. He had been instructed in all the duties of knighthood. Soon he would go forth, helping the poor, relieving distress, and keeping always before him the hope of the Grail.

When he reached twenty-one, a great and solemn ceremony was held. He received the full honors of knighthood. He was given the golden spurs, and a wondrous red robe. Then with sword and shield he set forth on the great adventure.

A strange story is told about the sword and shield that Sir Galahad carried in his search for the Grail. It is said that the sword was found with the hilt projecting from a large block of red granite. The young knight placed his hand upon the hilt and drew upon it. Lo! It came smoothly forth. Moreover, when he placed it in the scabbard which he carried it fitted exactly.

The shield is said to have been left by his ancestors in an old church. There it had lain for centuries. None had been able to see it until Sir Galahad came.

Early in his travels, Sir Galahad met first with King Arthur and the knights of the Round Table. He found them in solemn session, for it had been foretold, that, on that very day, a knight would come who was destined to find the Grail.

While King Arthur and his court were discussing the strange prophecy Sir Galahad appeared in their midst. The king and his knights hastened to welcome him. They believed that the prophecy was fulfilled, that this was in truth, the young knight who was destined to succeed in his search for the Grail. So firm were many of the knights in their belief that they were eager to accompany him.

As Sir Galahad continued his journey, he came one day to an enchanted castle. This was the "Castle of the Grail." It was here that the Grail was believed to be hidden. He found the king and all his household held under the magic spell. They had been waiting for years for the perfect knight to come and free them.

Galahad had not yet, however, learned enough wisdom to break the mystic spell. He was compelled to ride away leaving the king and his household still under the power of the enchanter.

After wandering for many years, and growing wiser and wiser year by year, he one day returned to the enchanted castle. This time he spoke the words of wisdom! The power of the enchanter was broken! The king and his people were set free! He was then called—"Galahad the Deliverer."

Galahad, however, did not yet possess the cup. He beheld only a vision of it in the castle. Now he rides forth to find and possess it.

See the youthful knight! Clad in a bright red robe, his banner flying from his lance, he sets out on his holy quest. About him stand his friends, delivered from the terrible enchantment. In the foreground kneels the maiden, who, under the magic spell, had grown loathsome and ugly. Now her former beauty has been restored. In gratitude she kneels, and breathes a prayer as the knight rides forth.

The others stand with expressions of mingled awe and gratitude. In the background are the homes of these friends, and beyond, a glimpse of the sea toward which Sir Galahad rides.

The knight sits erect, his face to the future, his thought fixed upon the great adventure. The gallant charger seems to understand all that is in his master's mind. With intelligent eyes, arched neck, and confident spirit he moves forward. We know he will carry Sir Galahad to his goal!

Note the contrast made by the red of Sir Galahad's robe against the snow-white steed. This gives emphasis to the picture-pattern. The artist chose his brightest color and made his sharpest contrasts to emphasize the "center of interest."

For centuries *red* and *white* have represented certain ideas. Red always means "love of truth" and "zeal for right." *White* always means "purity." So, you see, the artist chose these colors for the "center of interest" because they help to tell the story. The *red* tells us that Sir Galahad was brave and confident in his "love of truth" and "his zeal for right." The *white* proclaims the "purity" of his character and purpose.

Sir Galahad and his snow-white steed stand strongly forth from the background. They are most important! Next, in importance, is the kneeling maiden. She helps to complete the group of light figures against the dark background.

See the quiet tones in the robes of the grateful friends! See the grayed hues of their houses. These make a very peaceful background for the "center of interest."

The rich red of Sir Galahad's robe, the white of his steed, and the light figure of the maiden make a beautiful pattern of color against this dark background. The picture, you see, is a decoration worked out in the form of design.

See the strong horizontal accents, the flying banner, its long red center, the red trappings of the horse, the dark folds across the maiden's dress! These horizontal accents make the picture peaceful and quiet.

See the strong vertical accents—the rider, the lance, the kneeling maiden!

They give dignity and strength to the pattern. And too, the artist wanted us to feel the strength of Sir Galahad's character, so he chose the vertical accents. Like the color, they too, help to tell the story of the brave young knight.

Though the story of Sir Galahad dates back to the days of knighthood, the great idea in the story belongs to our own time as well. It pictures the endless struggle between right and wrong.

THE STORY OF THE ARTIST

Edwin Austin Abbey is famous for his series of beautiful wall decorations in the Boston Public Library. "The Quest of the Holy Grail" is his most celebrated work. Happy are we in America to possess it!

Although Mr. Abbey is an American,

he lived in England for many years. He was born in Philadelphia in 1852. After making England his home, he returned only occasionally to this country.

This celebrated American artist began his art studies in the Pennsylvania Academy of Fine Arts. Here he rapidly developed as an illustrator. He seemed to possess the happy faculty of taking any old-time story and creating for it an entirely new type of illustration. As he grew older this talent became more marked.

When he was still quite young, his beautiful illustrations had attracted the attention of publishers. When he was nineteen, Harper and Brothers of New York City sent him to England to gather material for illustrating a series of poems.

It was while on this visit that young Mr. Abbey became so charmed with rural England that he decided to make that country his home.

Mr. Abbey won his greatest success as a teller of stories. He especially enjoyed interesting historical tales for they furnished costumes and settings that added to the beauty of the illustrations.

Consequently when he was invited to decorate the walls of the Boston Public Library he naturally chose a story that would lend itself to beautiful illustration.

He had read the story of the Grail many times. It had made a deep impression upon his artistic imagination. It brought many pictures to his mind. Moreover, this story from the period of knighthood furnished the costumes, mediaeval castles, and church interiors, in which he delighted. Further, the story of the Grail had been sung by the poets of both England and America. From every point of view, the story of Sir Galahad and his search for the Grail was, indeed, a very worthy field for Mr. Abbey's very unusual story-telling powers.

After deciding upon this subject for his decoration, he gave all his time to study and preparation for the work. He studied the costumes of the Middle Ages, the armor of knights, ancient castles, and the meaning of color.

Seven years passed before the work was completed. In a series of panels he tells the story of the hero, Sir Galahad, who finally succeeded in the search for the Grail. The pictures are eight feet high but vary in length. One, "The Castle of the Grail," is thirty-three feet long and fills the entire length of the wall.

Every day brings many visitors to the Boston Library; among them are the boys and girls of the city who come to exchange their books. Before these pleasing decorations they stand, reading through pictures, the story of the peerless knight, Sir Galahad.

While still at work on this painting the artist was called to England by

King Edward VII, and invited to paint the great picture of the coronation scene. This, too, was another work in which beautiful costumes and groupings played an important part.

While in England he became very popular. Many honors were conferred upon him. He is one of the few American artists who have become famous abroad as well as at home.

DIRECTED STUDY

1. What was the Grail?
   Why was it sought?

2. Who was destined to succeed in the quest of the Grail?
   To what famous Order did he belong?

3. Tell the story of his sword.
   Tell the story of his shield.

4. What qualities of character were required?
   Did he succeed immediately in his adventure?

5. Why is he called "Galahad the Deliverer"?
   Describe his figure. His face. His dress.
   Describe the steed. Its spirit.
   Is there feeling in common between horse and rider? What?

6. How does the picture-pattern express the character of the young knight?
   Who is the artist?
   Where was he born? When?
   What was his great gift?
   Where is this famous decoration?

Related Music: PROCESSIONAL OF KNIGHTS—Parsifal ..
................*Wagner*

PRONUNCIATION OF PROPER NAMES

ABBEY .... (ăb′ ĭ)

ARTZ .... (ärts)

BRETON, JULES (zhōōl brẽ′ tôn′)

DALLIN .... (dăl′ in)

DELFT .... (dĕlft)

GRABAR, IGOR. (ē′ gor gră bär′)

INNESS .... (ĭn′ ĕs)

KATWYK .... (kät vīk)

LENINGRAD ..... (lĕ nēn′ gräd)

SOROLLA .... (sō rōl yä)

VALENCIA....... (vä lĕn shēä)

VERMEER, JAN.. (yän fâr mâr′)

STUCK, Frans von..............
.... (frănz fŏn stŏŏk)

SUGGESTIONS TO TEACHERS

STUDYING THE PICTURE. Any picture presented for study becomes more interesting when freely discussed in a natural way by the class. Before reading the text it is always advisable to study the picture. Pupils should be encouraged to give their own impressions; tell what they like in a picture; and WHY they like it.

In the intermediate and grammar grades simple elements in picture-making may be pointed out,—i.e. light and shade, repetition of line, of color, color harmony, balance, and center of interest. Such questions as,—From what direction does the light come? Where does it shine brightest? — and others of a similar nature, may help the pupil to SEE. Led by the teacher's skillful questioning, pupils gradually acquire the ability to discover for themselves many elements of design in picture-making.

DRAMATIZATION. Many of the pictures used in the intermediate and grammar grades lend themselves to dramatization. Under no circumstances is it necessary to burden one's self, in the class room, with an exact reproduction. The details of costume are not required. Any outstanding accessory of dress, easily at hand, may, however, add interest. It is the pose of the figure, the grouping if there are several, and the action, that are best appreciated by the pupils when the effort is made to reproduce a picture.

CORRELATION. Many of the famous pictures of this series bear directly upon interesting historical events. These, in particular, furnish subjects for language and composition.

Drawing lessons may with real profit be given over to the tracing of pictures, for the purpose of studying line, composition, light and shade.

The music hour offers still another

opportunity for related study. Pictures, like music, create emotions. When possible in the study of pictures, add the music which suggests the spirit and atmosphere of the picture. THE INTEREST IS ALWAYS KEENLY STIMULATED WHEN PORTIONS FROM VARIOUS SELECTIONS ARE PLAYED, AND THE CHILDREN PERMITTED TO CHOOSE THE ONE BEST SUITED TO THE PICTURE.

The suggestions for musical selections, which follow the questions on the picture, will be of great value to the teacher.

As far as possible, each pupil should own his own pictures. This leads to the making of picture-study books, envelopes, and folders, for preserving his pictures.

STUDY OF ARTISTS. Many times when studying an artist, children are delighted to bring to the class room other reproductions of his pictures.

This always stimulates interest. With several pictures by the same artist before the class, the outstanding characteristics of the painter, whether in color, composition, or some other phase of picture-making, may be intelligently discussed by the pupils. After such study as this, what "Millet" or "Rembrandt" will not be instantly recognized!

Sometimes pictures of the same subject by different artists is an equally interesting form of study. Such a series under a general subject, — as "Knighthood," "Trees," "Boats," "Joan of Arc"—affords many opportunities for valuable comparisons. Children will readily discover that each of the artists, treating the same subject, tells his story in a different way. This cultivates intelligent SEEING, and appreciation.

Free discussion of pictures before the class are always vital to real enjoyment of the masterpieces.

To be introduced in early years to the masterpieces of the ages, and to learn of the kingly minds who have ruled in this realm of beauty, is sure to develop an interest which will enlarge, enrich, and refine the future life of the pupil.